THE HISTORY OF THE AMERICAN REVOLUTION

A History Book for New Readers

Written by
Emma Carlson Berne

Illustrated by
Angie Alape

ROCKRIDGE PRESS

To Henry, Leo, and Oscar, my in-house American history buffs

For general information on our other products and services or to obtain technical support, please contact our Customer Care Department within the United States at (866) 744-2665, or outside the United States at (510) 253-0500.

Rockridge Press publishes its books in a variety of electronic and print formats. Some content that appears in print may not be available in electronic books, and vice versa.

Series Designer: Angela Navarra
Interior and Cover Designer: Stephanie Sumulong
Art Producer: Hannah Dickerson
Editor: Eliza Kirby
Production Editor: Nora Milman
Production Manager: Martin Worthington

Paperback ISBN: 978-1-64876-791-3 | eBook ISBN: 978-1-63807-821-0
R0
Printed in China

CONTENTS

CHAPTER 1

SETTING THE STAGE

Understanding the American Revolution

Paul Revere bent over the neck of his galloping horse. His overcoat was blowing out behind him in the night air. The horse's hooves pounded the muddy dirt road. The moon shone on the cornfields. Ahead, Paul could see the dark houses of Lexington.

It was April 18, 1775, and British army troops were marching toward Lexington, Massachusetts. They were coming to arrest Samuel Adams and John Hancock. Paul had come to warn them. Panting, he stopped in front of the house where Samuel and John were sleeping. He shouted, "The British are coming! Now!" Inside, someone lit a candle. Samuel and John scrambled into their clothes. Paul leaned his head on his horse's neck. He had delivered the message. The American Revolution was about to begin.

Britain and the American **colonists** weren't always at war. For many years, the settlers of the 13 **colonies** were happy living in America and being ruled by the British king, George III. They thought the rules the king made were mostly fair.

Everything changed in 1763. King George's government had borrowed a lot of money to

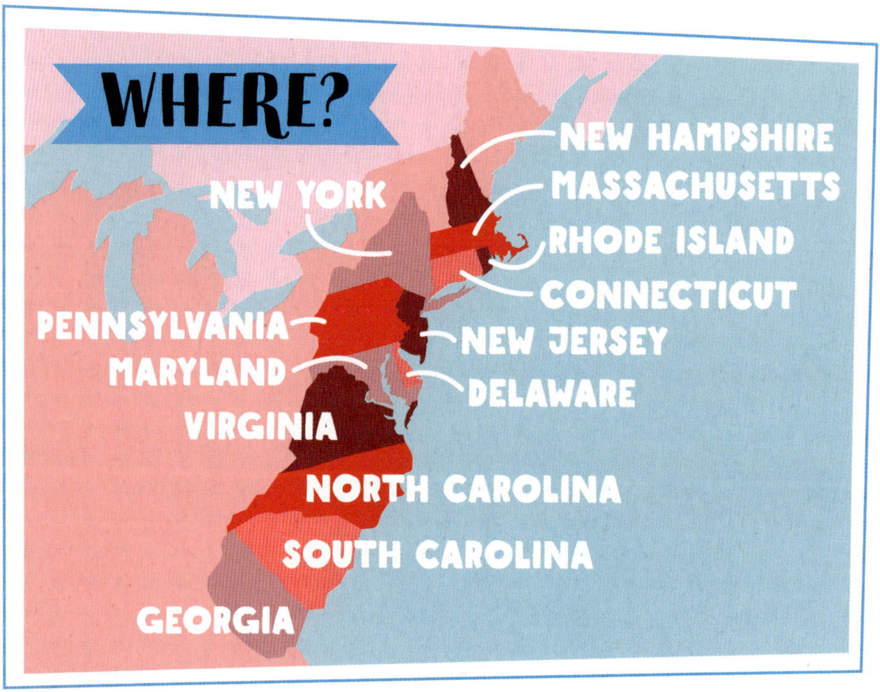

fight a war against the French in America. Britain had won, but now they needed money to pay back their giant **debts**. How did they decide to get it? They put **taxes** on goods the colonists bought.

The colonists were furious at having to pay high taxes on tea, paper, glass, and other supplies. They decided to fight back. From 1775 until 1783, Americans fought in Virginia, Massachusetts, and New York for freedom from Britain. This is their story.

JUMP -IN THE- THINK TANK

Can you think of reasons why someone would want to leave their homeland and move across the ocean to start a new colony and way of life?

Life in the American Colonies

When the revolution started, the colonists had been living in America for more than 150 years. Britain had been setting up more and more colonies. Eventually, there were

13 colonies: Massachusetts, Virginia, New York, New Hampshire, Rhode Island, Connecticut, New Jersey, Pennsylvania, Delaware, Maryland, North Carolina, South Carolina, and Georgia. They were located along what is now the East Coast of the United States. The colonists moved into land that **Indigenous** Peoples had lived on for thousands of years.

The colonists cut down trees and built cabins to live in. They hunted and grew crops to eat. The colonists also grew tobacco, corn, and rice to send back to Britain. **Enslaved** African people were forced to work on the huge farms, especially in the southern colonies.

The colonists didn't have a regular **military** to protect themselves. America wasn't a country, and only countries had armies. Instead, the colonies had groups of volunteers called **militias**. These were groups of men from the same area. They would sometimes meet to practice with their weapons. But they weren't a big, trained army like the British forces.

Britain—and King George III—made all the decisions for the colonies. Even though they lived in America, the colonists were supposed to obey the British government. No matter what the king ordered, the colonists had to follow his rules.

Many people in the colonies were not rich. They were focused on growing enough food to feed their families. They did not have extra money to spend on paying taxes to Britain. When the British government ordered the colonists to do unfair things, they were supposed to obey—and they did. Still, the colonists were getting angrier and angrier.

WHO?

King George III was the King of England for 60 years. He led Britain during the American Revolution. He died at the age of 81 in 1820.

WHEN?

The first American colony, Virginia, is founded.

1607

The last of the 13 colonies, Georgia, is founded.

1733

CHAPTER 2

THE COLONIES REBEL

☆ Paying the Price ☆

Britain and France fought a war in North America for seven years—from 1754 to 1763. The war was called the French and Indian War. France joined forces with the Indigenous Peoples, who were called Indians at the time, to fight against Britain. Britain and France each wanted to control more of the new land.

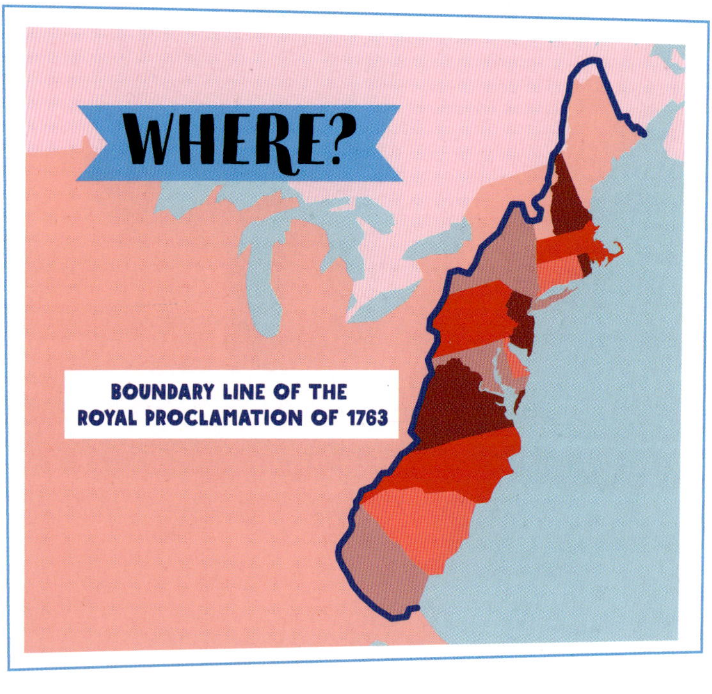

Britain won, but after, they needed a lot of money to pay their debts from the war. They passed the Royal Proclamation of 1763. This law said that colonists couldn't build farms on the land the British had won. Many colonists had already settled on that land. Now they had to leave, even though they didn't want to.

The colonists were angry. They wanted a chance to build farms on the new land. What's more, Britain ordered the colonists to pay a brand-new tax. The British government passed the Stamp Act in 1765. This law said that every time the colonists bought paper, playing cards, or other **documents**, they had to pay extra money to the British government.

The colonists thought this tax was very unfair. They did not have a lot of money. Now Britain wanted to charge them for using paper! If a farmer wanted to sell a plow to his neighbor, he had to pay a tax just to write the sale on a piece of paper.

That was not the only tax. In 1767, the British government passed the Townshend Acts. The law said that colonists had to pay extra money for paints, glass, and tea. The colonists had nobody to speak up for them in the British government. They didn't have someone from *their* side in **Parliament**. Some colonists began to think they might be better off without Britain.

Boston Fights Back

Not everyone in the colonies was angry with Britain. Plenty of people still supported the king and the British government. But more and more did not. Many of these **rebels** lived in Boston, Massachusetts. They had meetings, wrote **pamphlets** against the Townshend Acts, and printed newspapers saying that Britain was being unfair to the colonists.

The rebels decided to stop buying the things that Britain was taxing. This made Britain angry. They sent soldiers to patrol the streets of Boston so they could keep an eye on the colonists. The colonists and soldiers would argue often. Everyone was tense. On March 5, 1770, some colonists got into a fight with the British soldiers. The soldiers shot five of them. The newspapers called this fight the "Boston **Massacre**." The colonists were filled with rage.

Britain decided to take away the taxes on glass, paints, and paper, but they kept the tax on tea. Tea was very important to the colonists.

JUMP
-IN THE-
THINK TANK

What are some other ways the colonists could have shown Britain how unfair the tea tax was?

Everyone drank tea. The colonists wanted this unfair tax taken away, too.

On December 16, 1773, the colonists fought back. They planned an event called the Boston Tea Party. When ships carrying tea arrived from Britain, a group of rebels boarded the boats. They opened the tea crates and dumped all the tea into the water. The tea was ruined. Now no one could buy British tea—or pay taxes on it. The rebels' demands were clear: End the unfair taxes and remove the British troops—or else!

WHO?

Samuel Adams led rebels in many **protests** before the American Revolution began. He also helped plan the Boston Tea Party. Later, Samuel Adams signed the Declaration of Independence.

WHEN?

- **FEBRUARY 1763** — The French and Indian War ends.
- **OCTOBER 1763** — The Royal Proclamation is passed.
- **1765** — Parliament passes the Stamp Act.
- **1767** — The Townshend Acts are passed.
- **1770** — Five colonists are shot during the Boston Massacre.
- **1773** — The Boston Tea Party takes place.

CHAPTER 3

REVOLUTION!

The First Continental Congress

After the Boston Tea Party, the British government came down even harder on the rebel colonists. In 1774, they passed what came to be known as the Intolerable Acts. These acts made life difficult for the colonists. The port of Boston was closed. Ships could not come or go, which made it hard to get supplies.

Colonists could not decide how to run their own towns anymore. The British government decided everything. British soldiers could also live in colonists' homes—whenever they wanted. They watched what the colonists did and said. Then they reported what they saw and heard to Britain.

But the colonists weren't finished fighting back. They refused to accept the Intolerable Acts, just like they refused to accept the Stamp Act and the Townshend Acts. In 1774, they called a big meeting—the First Continental Congress. George Washington, John Adams, and other colonial leaders gathered in Philadelphia to write a **petition** to King George III. They asked him to take away the Intolerable Acts.

King George III never even replied to the petition. The Intolerable Acts stayed in place. The colonists were completely under British control.

The colonial leaders were moving closer and closer to battle with Britain. They just didn't

know how they would do it. Britain's army was one of the richest, best trained in the world. They had piles of uniforms and weapons—**muskets** and **bayonets**. They could buy all the food and supplies their soldiers would need. The colonists had no army at all. They didn't have any uniforms or bayonets. But they were determined to fight back.

JUMP —IN THE— THINK TANK

The colonists' army needed uniforms and weapons. What else would a brand-new army need to fight against the British?

The Shot Heard 'Round the World

The British knew the colonists were getting ready to fight. On the night of April 18, 1775, the British set out to arrest Samuel Adams and John Hancock near Lexington, Massachusetts. But Paul Revere warned the rebel leaders during his wild ride, and they escaped.

WHO?

Paul Revere wasn't the only nighttime rider during the revolution. On April 26, 1777, Sybil Ludington rode her horse 40 miles to warn troops of a British attack near Danbury, Connecticut. She was only 16 years old.

Word spread and the colonial militia was waiting when the British arrived in Lexington. Everyone knew a battle was coming. Someone fired first. No one knows who. Then the British fired their guns, killing eight **minutemen**. They marched to the nearby town of Concord. Then they destroyed guns and gunpowder the colonists were storing there.

The British began marching the 12 miles back to Boston. But the minutemen were ready. They hid in barns, behind fences, and up in trees. They fired on the British from their hiding spots.

They snuck through the woods where the British could not see them, and fired again. The British were not used to this way of fighting. They were used to soldiers meeting each other and fighting in the open. The minutemen killed many British soldiers, even though the British had more guns and more men.

After the battle, the colonists heard about the minutemen's victory. Many people couldn't believe the minutemen had actually beat the British.

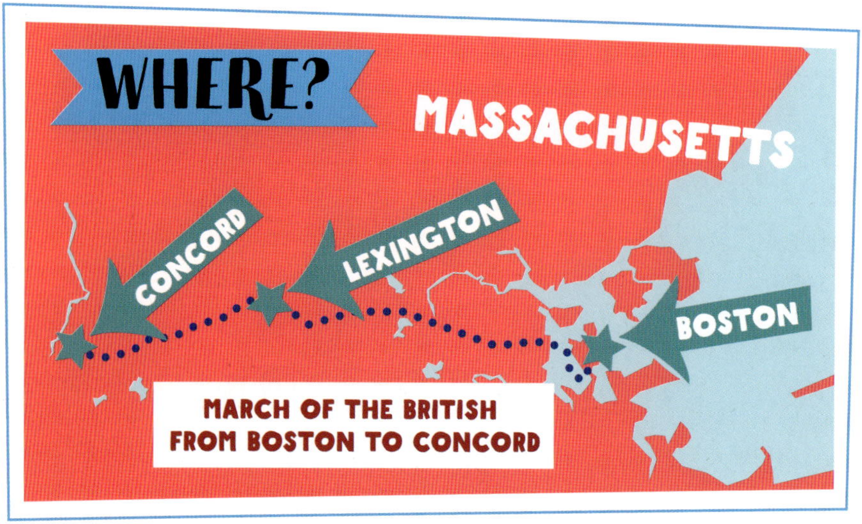

They began to think that maybe—just maybe—the rebels could actually fight a war against the British and win.

WHEN?

MARCH 1774	SEPTEMBER 1774	1775
The Intolerable Acts are passed.	The First Continental Congress meets.	Troops fight the Battles of Lexington and Concord.

CHAPTER 4

COMING TOGETHER

The Second Continental Congress

Now that muskets had been fired, the colonies needed to get ready for battle. The colonial leaders met again in May 1775 for the Second Continental Congress in Philadelphia. The colonies needed two important things for the coming war against Britain: an army and someone to lead it.

The leaders agreed to use the militia in Boston as their army. They would also look for more men to join. They picked George Washington as the commander in chief. Washington was from Virginia. He was already a colonial leader. He had fought in the French and Indian War, so he knew how to command an army. He was strong and the soldiers trusted him.

Meanwhile, the rebel militias and the British troops were still fighting in the woods and fields around Boston. In June, the minutemen surrounded the city of Boston. They wanted to defend it from British attacks. This left the towns outside Boston with no protection. The British marched to those areas, but the minutemen learned of their plans. They hurried to the unprotected areas and got ready.

The British showed up at Bunker Hill the next morning. The minutemen were waiting for them at the top. As the British marched up

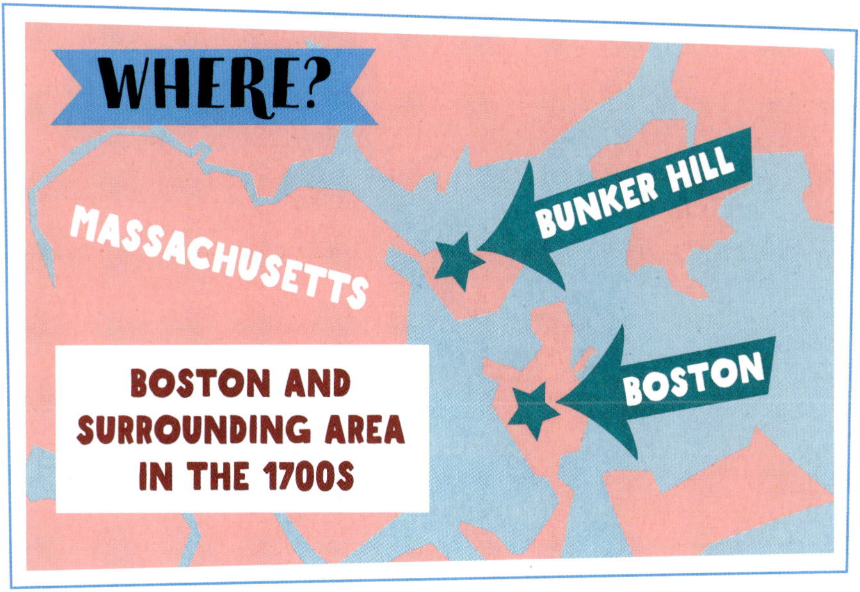

the hill, the minutemen fired their muskets. Again and again, gunfire rang out. The British pressed forward. Finally, the British drove the minutemen off the hill. They had won, but lost a lot of soldiers—many more than the Americans. The British learned that the minutemen were surprisingly good fighters. The colonial militias learned they could hold their own against the British army, win or lose.

Washington's Army

George Washington had a lot of work to do. The colonists were already formed into small groups. Washington needed to join all those groups together into one big army. The soldiers had never fought together in a real military. Washington had to teach them how.

Soldiers in the **Continental Army** got up at dawn. When they were not fighting, the men dug trenches, cleared trees, or built forts.

WHO?

George Washington was a rich farmer from Virginia. He was 43 years old when he became leader of the Continental Army. After the war, George Washington became the first president of the United States.

They practiced shooting and guarded the camps. They ate one hot meal a day, usually beef and bread. Soldiers put any leftover food in their packs for later. They also carried a bowl, spoon, blanket, water canteen, and paper for writing letters.

JUMP -IN THE- THINK TANK

How do you think the Continental soldiers felt as they prepared for war? Scared, excited, worried, or glad? Why do you think they may have felt each of these things?

The soldiers put great effort into keeping their gunpowder dry. Wet gunpowder would not work, which meant the soldier could not fire his musket during battle.

Free Black men fought in the army. Some fought in Black units, and some in mixed white-Black units. George Washington enslaved more than 100 Black people on his own farm. He brought an enslaved person, William Lee, to help him during the war. Other enslaved Black people also fought in their own units. Many Indigenous tribes offered their warriors. The Penobscot and the Passamaquoddy tribes sent hundreds of their men to fight alongside the white colonists.

Washington had his army. By March 1776, he had forced the British out of Boston.

He had control of that important city. No one knew what the British might do next—or if the Continental Army could stand up to them.

WHEN?

MAY 1775	JUNE 1775	MARCH 1776
The Continental Congress agrees to go to war.	The Battle of Bunker Hill is fought.	The Continental Army drives the British from Boston.

CHAPTER 5

BATTLING FOR INDEPENDENCE

The Declaration of Independence

While the soldiers were fighting, colonists were talking. About what? Independence! Ordinary people read about it in the newspapers. They also chatted about it with their families at home and with their friends in the streets. Many of them had read a pamphlet called *Common Sense* by the thinker Thomas Paine. Thomas Paine wrote simply and clearly about the need for independence. People are born equal, he wrote, and no one is a ruler over another.

The colonial leaders saw that many colonists wanted to become independent from Britain. When the Second Continental Congress met again in Philadelphia in June 1776, they made an important decision. They decided to officially declare the colonies' independence from Britain. To do this, they needed a document.

WHO?

Thomas Jefferson was a writer, farmer, and politician from Virginia. Jefferson kept many enslaved Black people on his farm, Monticello. He was America's third president, from 1801 to 1809.

The leaders asked Thomas Jefferson, Benjamin Franklin, John Adams, and a few others to create one.

The group chose Jefferson to do most of the writing. He wrote and rewrote what they had to say. When the Continental Congress read his first draft, they argued about some of the words he used. Jefferson made changes. Finally, the Congress voted to accept the Declaration of Independence. It passed the vote. On July 4, 1776, they declared that the United States was its own free nation. They sent a copy of the Declaration to King George III. The United States was now officially at war with Britain.

Life in the Army

The Continental Army kept Boston safe from the British. It wasn't easy. They were still fighting the strongest army on the planet. The British focused on another big city—New York. In August 1776, the British navy sailed into New York Harbor.

JUMP IN THE THINK TANK

Imagine you are writing the Declaration of Independence. What words would you use? How would you begin? What thoughts would you make sure to include?

So many British soldiers marched and fought their way through the city that the Continental Army was forced to leave.

Hundreds of American soldiers were killed. George Washington cried as he watched the living soldiers leave New York. Washington knew he had to do something bold. Many of his men didn't believe they could win against the British. This was Washington's last chance to convince them they could.

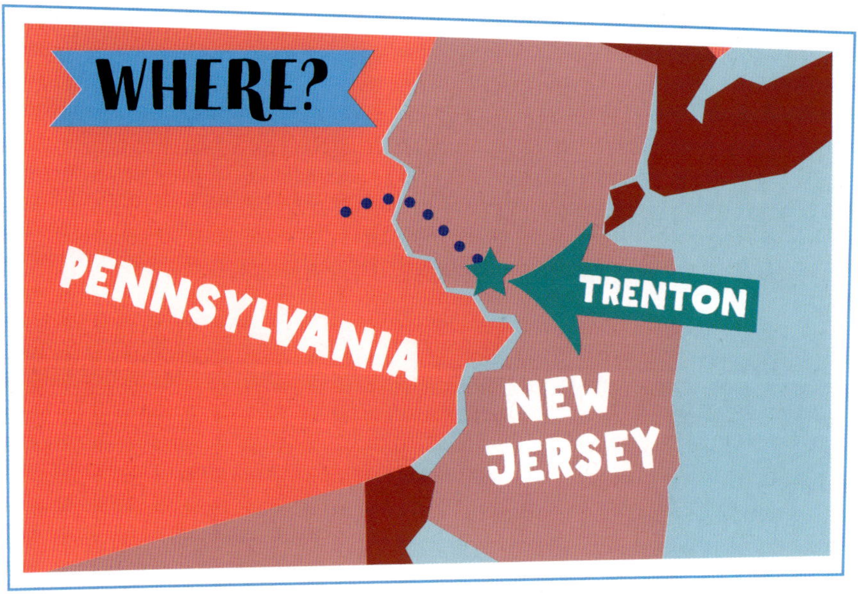

On Christmas day in 1776, George Washington led the Continental Army to the Delaware River. The wind was howling. Snow and sleet pelted the men's faces. Some didn't even have shoes to wear as they marched through the snow. They quietly paddled boats from Pennsylvania's shore and crossed the ice-filled water of the river.

Once across, they snuck up to the fort of Trenton in New Jersey. The British soldiers were spending the winter there. The Continental Army attacked the soldiers resting inside.

The British were caught by surprise, and the Americans fought hard. When the battle was over, the Americans had won.

It was the victory the Continental Army needed. They had captured a fort that was well-protected. Only a few American soldiers had been killed. Leaders from around the world saw that Washington was a good general. The colonists saw that their army *could* fight and win.

WHEN?

JULY 1776	SEPTEMBER 1776	DECEMBER 1776
The Declaration of Independence is accepted.	The British army captures New York.	The Continental Army captures Trenton.

CHAPTER 6

A SHOCKING VICTORY

A Helping Hand

Other countries watched the American Revolution carefully. They wanted to see if the new country would be worth supporting. In autumn 1777, the Continental Army had a chance to prove that they were.

British troops were in Canada, hoping to attack the northern colonies. Major General Benedict Arnold, an American army leader, had heard the British were going to attack. He waited with the American troops near the town of Saratoga, New York. Then the British made their move.

WHO?

Benedict Arnold was a military leader in the Continental Army. In 1780, he decided to leave the American side and fight for the British. The Americans were never able to capture him.

The two armies fought hard. Many soldiers on both sides died. The British won the battle, but barely. They had lost so many men that they needed to send for more troops. They waited and waited for them to arrive. The Americans waited, too.

Finally, the British commanders decided they couldn't wait for the new troops any longer. They attacked the Americans near Saratoga. The Americans were ready. They fought back, and won. The British **surrendered**.

But the war wasn't over. The Continental Army lost other battles. Winter was coming and Washington had to find a safe place for his troops to live. In December 1777, the army made camp at Valley Forge, Pennsylvania.

At the camp, the tired, sick, and starving soldiers huddled around campfires in the snow. They had been fighting for a year and a half.

JUMP —IN THE— THINK TANK

How could the American soldiers have helped each other during the winter at Valley Forge? How could their leaders have helped them?

They didn't have enough food or warm clothes. Many of the soldiers were barefoot.

Finally, good news came in the spring. After the Battle of Saratoga, the country of France decided to support the American side of the war. They sent money, weapons, battleships, and troops. The French gave the Continental Army the things they needed to keep fighting.

☆ Waving the White Flag ☆

The war went on for four more long years. The Continental soldiers were tired of fighting. The colonists were tired of the fighting, too. By 1781, Washington knew the American people might stop supporting the war. He knew he needed to win a big victory—soon!

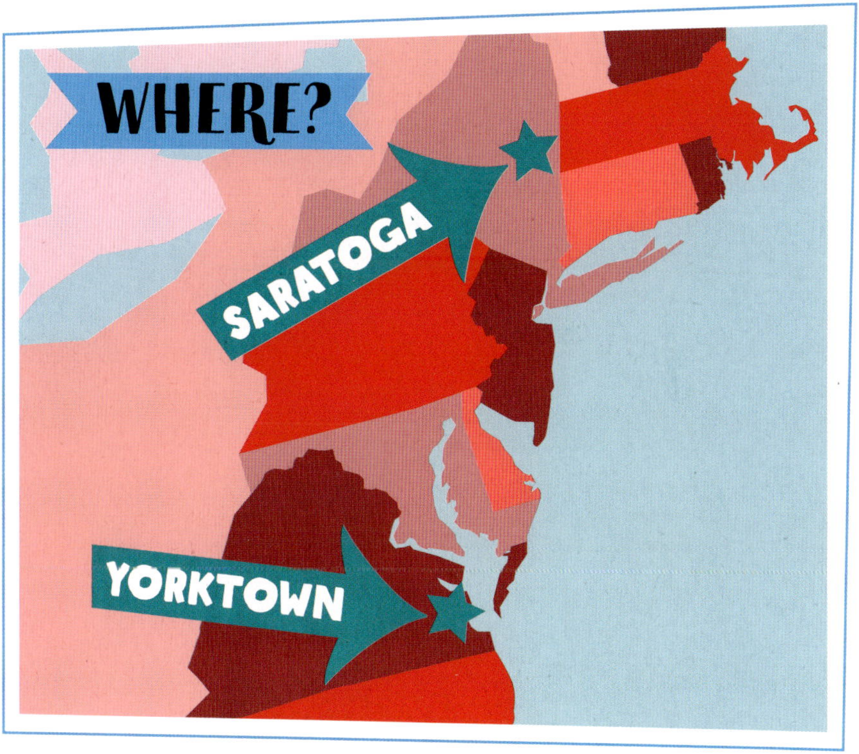

When the British army made camp near Yorktown, Virginia, Washington saw his chance. In September 1781, he led troops to the British camp. There, the American troops surrounded the British so they couldn't leave their camp. The American soldiers attacked again and again. They also kept anyone else from coming to help the British soldiers. Finally, on October 19, the British troops surrendered.

The British had lost about 24,000 soldiers over the course of the war. They had also lost many battles. To make things more difficult, America had powerful **allies** like the French now.

When they lost the Battle of Yorktown, the British realized the war was over.

Word of the surrender quickly spread throughout the colonies. Britain didn't hear until much later. The ships taking the message to British leaders took more than a month to sail to London. The colonists were stunned when they heard of the surrender. The British leaders were stunned, too. No one could believe that a brand-new army with barely any clothes or weapons could beat the strongest army in the world. Americans ran into the streets and sang and danced.

WHEN?

British and Continental troops fight at the Battle of Saratoga in New York.

SEPTEMBER-OCTOBER 1777

The Continental Army camps at Valley Forge, Pennsylvania.

DECEMBER 1777

The British surrender to the Americans after losing the Battle of Yorktown on October 19.

1781

CHAPTER 7

THE UNITED STATES OF AMERICA

The Treaty of Paris

America did not declare victory right away. Benjamin Franklin, John Adams, and another colonial leader named John Jay went to France. They spent a lot of time talking with the British leaders to come up with a peace **treaty**. The Americans wanted the British to admit that the United States was independent. This would let them make deals with other countries. The leaders also talked about where the borders of the new country would be. The American leaders wanted to settle land in the west.

WHO?

Benjamin Franklin was an inventor, writer, and thinker who also helped write the Declaration of Independence, the Treaty of Paris, and the Constitution. He invented the lightning rod and bifocals, a type of eyeglasses.

Finally, almost two years after the war ended, the Treaty of Paris was signed on September 3, 1783. The war was officially over. The United States of America was born! But the Americans still had work to do. They had to figure out just what kind of country they wanted to be. Who would lead them? How would people choose their leaders? What would their laws be?

All these questions and many more were discussed at the Constitutional Convention. This important meeting was held from May to September 1787. There, the leaders wrote the Constitution of the United States. The Constitution listed all the laws and rules of the brand-new country. It created the three branches, or parts, of government: the president, Congress, and the Supreme Court. On September 17, 1787, the leaders signed the Constitution.

The Birth of a New Nation

In 1789, two years after the Constitution was signed, George Washington was elected the first President of the United States. He had a lot to do. The war had left the new country with very little money. Congress could not even afford to pay the Continental Army soldiers their wages. In addition, slavery was still legal.

JUMP IN THE THINK TANK

After the revolution, enslaved Black people were still not free. How do you think the colonial leaders explained this?

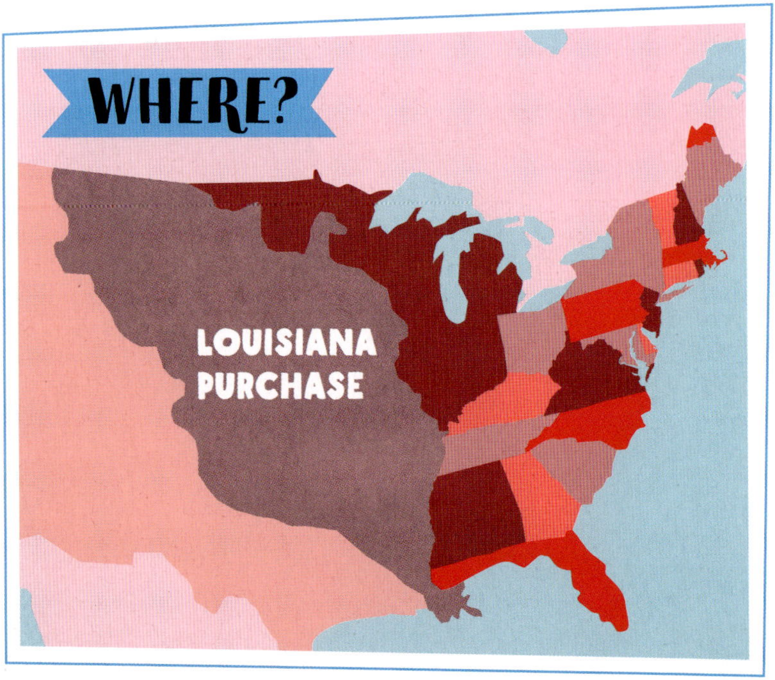

Northern and Southern states regularly argued whether or not people should still be enslaved in the new country.

The United States had gained both new freedoms and land. The first 10 amendments to the Constitution, known as the Bill of Rights, were put in place in 1791. They promised Americans the right to free speech, freedom of religion, and the right to publish their thoughts and opinions. The Treaty of Paris opened up big chunks of land in what is today the Midwest. More and more Americans left their homes and made the long journey to settle there.

As the years went by, the United States fought other wars, including the War of 1812 with the British. Americans fought each other during the Civil War. The government also fought wars against Indigenous Peoples. The government forced thousands to move from their homes as white pioneers settled the land out west.

Americans have never forgotten that they were not always free. The freedoms written in the Constitution and the Bill of Rights are special. Americans have always been proud

that they have the right to speak out against the government. The Continental Army and their leaders fought for these rights and many others. Their courage and strength helped make the United States the country it is today.

WHEN?

- **1783** — America and Britain sign the Treaty of Paris, ending the war.
- **MAY 1787** — The Constitutional Convention begins in Philadelphia.
- **SEPTEMBER 1787** — The Constitution is signed.
- **1812** — War of 1812 with Britain begins.
- **1861** — The Civil War begins.

CHAPTER 8

SO . . . WHAT'S THE HISTORY OF THE AMERICAN REVOLUTION?

Challenge Accepted!

Now that you have learned all about the American Revolution, let's test your new knowledge in a little who, what, when, where, why, and how quiz. Feel free to look back in the text to find the answers if you need to, but try to remember first!

1 What item did the Stamp Act tax?

- A Glass
- B Tea
- C Paper
- D Oxen

2 Fill in the blank:

The document Thomas Jefferson helped write is called The_____ of Independence.

- A Resolution
- B Demand
- C Explanation
- D Declaration

3 **Where did the colonial rebels dump tea during the Boston Tea Party?**

→ A In the Hudson River

→ B In Boston Harbor

→ C In the middle of the Atlantic Ocean

→ D In Lake Superior

4 **What was Thomas Paine's important pamphlet called?**

→ A *Common Sense*

→ B *Thinking Smart*

→ C *American Independence*

→ D *Britain's Wrongs*

5 **What season did the Continental Army spend at Valley Forge?**

→ A Winter

→ B Spring

→ C Summer

→ D Fall

6 **Who was the commander in chief of the Continental Army?**

- A Thomas Jefferson
- B Benedict Arnold
- C George Washington
- D Benjamin Franklin

7 **How did George Washington and the army cross the Delaware River on their way to Trenton?**

- A They marched across a bridge.
- B They swam.
- C They used stepping-stones.
- D They paddled in boats.

8 **Which country supported the Americans after the Battle of Saratoga?**

- A Spain
- B France
- C The Netherlands
- D Britain

9 **Where was the treaty signed that ended the American Revolution?**

- A Paris, France
- B Madrid, Spain
- C Philadelphia, Pennsylvania
- D London, Britain

10 **The American Revolution ended ____ in the United States.**

- A Slavery
- B Westward expansion
- C British rule
- D Violence

Answers: 1. C; 2. D; 3. B; 4. A; 5. A; 6. C; 7. D; 8. B; 9. A; 10. C

Our World

The American Revolution took place 250 years ago, but the lessons Americans learned during the war are still around today.

- → Americans really like that they can freely think and do what they want. They are not afraid to speak up and often **debate** with each other and their government.
- → The United States is one of the largest **democracies** in the world. It still has the three branches of government set up in the Constitution.
- → The United States has helped countries, such as Kuwait and Liberia, fight for their independence.

JUMP IN THE THINK TANK FOR MORE!

Pretend you are living in colonial times. Imagine that you are a soldier or a colonist in these situations.

→ Imagine that you are a farmer and you're asked to fight with the Continental Army. If you do, your family might not be able to harvest the crops on time. What do you decide and why?

→ Pretend you are a soldier in Washington's army at Valley Forge. What are the top five things you need to get you through the hard winter?

→ Imagine you are a British soldier during the surrender at Yorktown. Are you sad about losing the war? Are you calm? Angry?

Glossary

ally: A country that is friends with another country

bayonet: A blade attached to the end of a musket

colonist: A settler or person who lives in a colony

colony: An area apart from a country that is still controlled by that country

Continental Army: The American army during the American Revolution

debate: An argument about a topic from opposite sides

debt: Money that is owed back to the person it was borrowed from

democracy: A type of government that is made up of leaders chosen by the people of that country

document: A piece of writing that is used as an official record

enslave: To force a person to work without giving them freedom to choose and without paying them for their service

Indigenous: Original to a place; native

massacre: When many people are killed at the same time

military: The army of a country; trained soldiers

militia: An army of people who are not trained soldiers

minutemen: Members of the colonies who were ready to fight at a minute's notice in the period before and during the American Revolution

musket: A type of long gun

pamphlet: A small booklet about a certain subject

Parliament: The highest government in Britain, similar to Congress in the United States

petition: A request signed by many people and given to someone in charge

protest: To speak out against something

rebel: Someone who is against a ruler or a government

surrender: To give up

tax: Money that people must pay to a government

treaty: An agreement between countries

Bibliography

American Battlefield Trust. "Lexington and Concord: The Shot Heard 'Round the World." Accessed April 6, 2021. Battlefields.org/learn/articles/lexington-and-concord-shot-heard-round-world.

Ayres, Edward. "Yorktown and American Independence." Jamestown & American Revolution Settlement Museum at Yorktown. Accessed April 6, 2021. HistoryIsFun.org/yorktown-victory-center/yorktown-and-american-independence.

George Washington's Mount Vernon. "Battle of Saratoga." Accessed April 6, 2021. MountVernon.org/library/digitalhistory/digital-encyclopedia/article/battle-of-saratoga.

Independence National Historical Park (US National Park Service). "The Second Continental Congress and the Declaration of Independence." Accessed April 6, 2021. NPS.gov/inde/learn/historyculture/resources-declaration-secondcontinentalcongress.htm.

Gilder Lehrman Institute of American History. "The Stamp Act, 1765." Accessed April 6, 2021. GilderLehrman.org/history-resources/spotlight-primary-source/stamp-act-1765.

Massachusetts Historical Society. "The Battle of Bunker Hill." Accessed April 6, 2021. MassHist.org/revolution/bunkerhill.php.

National Archives. "The Declaration of Independence: How Did It Happen?" Accessed April 6, 2021. Archives.gov/founding-docs/declaration/how-did-it-happen.

NCC Staff. "From Hero to Traitor: Benedict Arnold's Day of Infamy." National Constitution Center. September 21, 2020. ConstitutionCenter.org/blog/from-hero-to-traitor-benedict-arnolds-day-of-infamy.

US Department of State Archive. "Treaty of Paris, 1783." Accessed April 6, 2021. 2001-2009.state.gov/r/pa/ho/time/ar/14313.htm.

Acknowledgments

I'd like to thank my editor, Eliza Kirby, for her thoughtful, efficient help as we worked through this seminal moment in American history together. I'm also grateful to the American Battlefield Trust for their thorough and excellent research on the history of the American Revolution, including its effects on enslaved and Indigenous Peoples. Lastly, I'm grateful to the rebels of the revolution, who saw injustice and fought back.

About the Author

Emma Carlson Berne has authored many books for young people, including *The Story of Anne Frank* (Rockridge Press, 2021) and *Books by Horseback* (Little Bee, 2021).

Emma lives in Cincinnati, Ohio, on land given to Continental Army soldiers after the end of the American Revolution. Emma often visits schools to speak about writing and the life of an author. She enjoys horseback riding, hiking, camping, and cooking. She is the mother of three boys and two cat-children. More about Emma and her books can be found at EmmaCarlsonBerne.com.

About the Illustrator

Angie Alape was born in Colombia. She grew up drawing on every cardboard box around her, making all kinds of nonexistent worlds to play in with her siblings. She has been working as a freelance illustrator since her first collaboration with a Chilean editorial; recently, she has worked in editorial publishing, social campaigns, character design for 3D animation, and web magazines. In her spare time, you can find her playing with her adopted dogs and looking for places to enjoy a nice meal over the weekend.